everyone
rides the bus
in a city
of losers

poems

jason freure

a misFit book

Get the
eBook free!*
*proof of purchase
required

Purchase the print edition
and receive the eBook free!
For details, go to ecwpress.com/eBook.

LIBRARY AND ARCHIVES CANADA
CATALOGUING IN PUBLICATION

Freure, Jason, author
Everyone rides the bus in a city of losers : poems /
Jason Freure.

A misFit book.
Issued in print and electronic formats.
ISBN 978-1-77041-453-2 (softcover).--
ALSO ISSUED AS: 978-1-77305-277-9 (ePUB),
978-1-77305-278-6 (PDF)

I. TITLE.

PS8611.R48E94 2018   C811'.6
C2018-902592-1   C2018-902593-X

Editor: Michael Holmes /
a misFit book

MISFIT

Cover design: Courtney Horner
Author photo: © Kaitlin Kealey

The publication of *Everyone Rides the Bus in a City of Losers* has been generously supported by the Canada Council for
the Arts which last year invested $153 million to bring the arts to Canadians throughout the country, and by the Government
of Canada. *Nous remercions le Conseil des arts du Canada de son soutien. L'an dernier, le Conseil a investi 153
millions de dollars pour mettre de l'art dans la vie des Canadiennes et des Canadiens de tout le pays. Ce livre est
financé en partie par le gouvernement du Canada.* We also acknowledge the Ontario Arts Council (OAC), an agency of
the Government of Ontario, and the contribution of the Government of Ontario through the Ontario Book Publishing Tax
Credit and the Ontario Media Development Corporation.

Ontario
Ontario Media Development
Corporation

ONTARIO ARTS COUNCIL
CONSEIL DES ARTS DE L'ONTARIO
an Ontario government agency
un organisme du gouvernement de l'Ontario

Canada Council
for the Arts

Conseil des Arts
du Canada

Canadä

PRINTED AND BOUND IN CANADA   PRINTING: COACH HOUSE PRINTING   5   4   3   2   1

ULTRAMAR

The last place I went was Ultramar.
I walked my friends there and said,
"You can hail a cab at Ultramar,"
the Ultramar where I bought ketchup chips
and Coffee Crisps and one time even Ringolos.

Only the night attendant knew my love of Swedish Berries
and plastic-wrapped smoked meats.
Only the night attendant who blasted *Appetite for Destruction*
knew my sweetheart's craze
for M&M's and Pez dispensers.

I bid my friends adieu at Ultramar.
They claimed Verdun was the middle of nowhere.
It's only the edge, I said to them.
Nowhere is somewhere west, out past the neon
5e Avenue on the New Verdun Diner.

My friends scrambled into taxis
shooting northward and eastward.
I bought a coffee at Ultramar.
I caught the night attendant air-guitaring.
I had to move by twelve o'clock.

LA ROCKETTE

No, I will never be as cool as the guy from Les Deuxluxes,
even if I buy him shots and quote his covers,
even if he says to me, "Look, man, all you need is a good friperie."
Will you never love me, Anna Frances Meyer?

But moustaches always made me think of arcade perverts
and my neighbours in Verdun.
After Nirvana played the Verdun Auditorium,
they found Courtney at Bar Côte St-Paul by the Cash'N'Loan.

When Jack White saved the Jack White Auditorium,
was it more Massey than Tony Wilson?
If she skips another shower, will the bartender at La Rockette
smell more like Durutti than raclette?

The guy from the band says that I should go.
But I won't go. Not until I meet Anna Frances Meyer.
Not until last call lights up the walls
and she finds me in the bathroom stall writing,
        "You just can't run, you just can't run from the funnel of love."

THE PEDESTRIAN

I have been walking for hours, stopped everywhere and not once sat
    down.
I was looking for something, but I couldn't find it at the comic book
    store.
The shelves made no sense, I couldn't tell titles from authors
and when the thing I wanted appeared I left it behind
because the clerk would judge me and all the wrong places I looked
with a look that meant, "I am looking for something and I know
    what it is,"
so I kept walking. I have been walking for hours.
I have stopped in so many espresso bars,
tried their microfoam concoctions and crema hearts.
I have sipped at each one and left before finding a table
because all the tables were taken, and I ordered "for here"
in their finger-scalding clay mugs, the diminutive ones
that come with plates and tiny handles and uncomfortable spoons,
but the tables were filled up with books and laptops and first dates
and long empty, killed cups, and no one needed to look up
or take their bookbags off their chairs, so I kept walking.
I walked north and south through avenues of beautiful houses
with their wrought iron tables-for-two on their second storey
    balconies
where ashtrays and coffee mugs and folded-open books
waited to be cleaned up. I did not stop to knock on their doors
or call the numbers on their "For Rent" signs. I could not afford them,
not even their attics, and because their bricks were old and
    overgrown
I didn't want to stay and envy children corralled in and out of their
    doors.
I hurled temper tantrums at their windows and bribed their cats to
    come home with me,
but the cats could smell the cheap food I would feed them,
so I kept walking, up wind and down river, on the lee side of
    skyscrapers,

through the valleys and ridges uptown where I forgot which way is
     up.
I walked into suds bars and tap rooms. I played their VLTs,
I sampled their eighteen beers, I listened to their patrons complain.
I heard them all out, about the music, about the service, about the
     extra half-inches of head.
Not once did I stay long enough to ask why they came back every
     day,
or ask the bartender what times they arrived or where they sat
when their favourite seats were occupied, why they lied about going
     to the gym.
No, I did not stay. I kept walking. I am still walking,
even though it's dark now and the lights in the houses are off
and the bars are closed until morning, and I do not stop in the
     diners,
I cannot decide if I am hungry or thirsty. I only know that I am tired,
I have been walking for many hours, my hair is matted with sweat
     and chisel dust,
I have been walking for many hours and do not know what I want
     anymore,
where I should stop or why, why I should ask for more
     disappointment,
why I should find a reason to hurry off again when I can keep
     walking.

CROSS ON MONT-ROYAL

Every evening at eight I turn my eyes to the cross and each time I
    hope that the pope has died.
Each time I ask myself how many minutes have passed since I last
    crossed a television
and what could have happened since then,
unless there's hockey that night, and then no one would know,
not even if Laval had floated out into the Atlantic, until ten o'clock.

Every evening at ten I turn my eyes to the cross and discover that
    the pope has not died,
he has abdicated.

Every evening, it is already midnight, and I will fall asleep if I read
    any more books.
I want to go out where there are all kinds of people checking on the
    pope's health.
They are sitting in the Sherbrooke metro station explaining how
    they were mugged.
They are racing through St-Louis Square with a little sway in their
    steps
because they stayed at the bar later than usual after work.
They are smoking in front of the nightclubs and they call me things
when I bump into them because I was on my tiptoes trying to peer
    over rooftops.

Every Friday and Saturday evening at one, I come out of the
    Sherbrooke metro station
after work and every time I expect the pope to have died.
He has never died once,
though the cross and the radio tower reassure me that up is still that
    way,
that I do have three or four friends and if I didn't, it wouldn't matter
because my gravy-slopping hand has improved a lot lately.

Every morning at five, I turn my eyes to the cross on Mont-Royal.
I can no longer tell how the pope is doing.
If it's winter and the overhead clouds are thick and bright
I sometimes mistake white for purple,
and I am thrilled for a moment, not because the pope has died,
because they have changed the colour of the cross to purple.

STILL LIFE WITH JUAN GRIS

I do not have a newspaper on my table.
I am not part of the newspaper generation.
There is one apple in my fruit bowl and many limes.

Le Devoir does not disappear under a fruit bowl
on my kitchen table. I do not scribble in *Le Devoir*'s margins.

The free weeklies pile up on my kitchen table for months.
How can I huddle at my kitchen table
when it does not sit next to a frozen window
and my floor is made of corrugated vinyl?

My kitchen table is next to an electric oven.
Grocery bags and dirty plates hoard my kitchen table.
I call it: *Studio frijole.*

Crumbs fill the crevices of my living room.
Broccoli rots on my kitchen table.

Cockroach, keep my dropped *frijoles*
but do not sneak up on my *paloma jimador*
when I drink at my kitchen table.

Why won't the grocer wrap my rib-eye in *Le Devoir*?
Black and white and bled all over. My rib-eyes can't breathe
in his Saran wrap.

Le Devoir sits on my table. Broccoli flourishes so beautifully
from my fruit bowl. A cockroach licks the ice in my *paloma
jimador* cocktail glass. Who ate my apple?

There is bleach on my kitchen table.
I burned the fruit bowl in the backyard.
I subscribed to *Le Devoir* dot-com.

SKETCHES AT LE CAGIBI

She practised microphones and yellow.
In the fauna of St-Viateur she is the lophiiformes
beaconing through deep aquatic nights.

CAFÉ RÉSONANCE

Graphite scratches heavy paper.
He has the alacrity of a spy—what if she caught his glances
at the slip of her off-the-shoulder shirt,
her expression of enjoying something?

I think I will be okay as long as he sketches.
I read to his pencil's shushing sweeps.
When I stand up I look over.
There I am in my silly shirt, face down in a book,
uncombed fjords of charcoal on my head.

ANNA WINTERS

She said I had nice shoes, but I was wearing red checkered Cons
coated in bar grime and winter. She looked like office lighting.
I looked for her at Korova, but they were dancing
between furtive trips to the restroom.
Their parkas were piled on the Pac-Man tables.
I could not find her red flannel among them
with the buttons on the men's side.
We met at Copa, while her friends and my friends flirted
and played pool, and she was not interested,
except she said I had nice shoes, I should take care of them.

I met her two weeks later. She was working at 3 Brasseurs
while I was wearing black checkered Cons with the tag tucked in my
    sock.
I told her I loved her, that I had searched Mile End for twelve days,
searched its ceilings and cellars, its launches and grand openings.
Her last words stick with me, like her mismatched hair,
"Eight percent is not a tip, you fucking creep,
and you should lint roll your coat, you look like a cat hoarder."

I can no more deny my friends than she can deny my eight percent,
not in times like these, when the frost comes down through the
    avenues
and the hydro bills ratchet toward an ugly spring.
She said her name was Winters. I would have caught her dandruff
    on my tongue.
"Winters. Anna Winters." From the high windows of Korova
I watch the drifts sweep the boulevard, leaping from mansards,
and the icicles that keep collapsing, skewering smokers,
shattering like my confidence that the groundhog is always wrong,
that the bartender will always keep my secrets, or even remember
    them.

MILE END

Bodies laugh in the dark bars.
I hear their glasses clink against wooden tables.
The fog in the windows hides their mouths
and how they contort into guffaws.
How many of them make video poems
of long alleys in the spring?
How many just work day jobs at Ubisoft?
I can't find the street signs through the melted snow
and wind tunnel tears.
I only find shadows of bodies
and the impression of warmth without feeling any.
Do they talk to themselves when they walk alone in the cold?
I ask the streets to repeat their secrets,
the things they mutter and chuckle
when they leave their jobs at five,
when they step into surprise afternoons
from the beds of their much-hipper Saturday lovers.
If I never meet the characters on Dieu du Ciel labels,
I may never come back to Mile End.
The snow is thick and so are the spaces
outside the valence of street lamps.
Once I'm sick of mysteries,
I won't venture over the CPR tracks anymore.
I won't risk that $146 ticket,
or pause to see the twenty pointing fingers from the viaduct.

SKETCHES AT LE CAGIBI

If there were more recipes for raw vegan nachos,
attendance could have been thin.
It was a poetry reading on Super Bowl Sunday.

ST-LAURENT BOULEVARD

I.

They hang around before meal times,
leaning over the pit
where the transport trucks fly eastbound
down Notre-Dame in the dirty cold.

"I see a Labatt forty in your future.
A whole two-four left out for recycling,
a long nap in the Champ-de-Mar tunnel.
Assault from a waiter,
gnawed duck bones and chicken feet.
Past the lions, wheeled clattering,
I hear 'five-oh, five-oh,'
an ungreased grind, houris up the hill,
the girlfriend you hit last summer
swinging round a lamp post
and smiling at strangers in the slush.
There is no change where the saints cross."

Frozen winds from the river.
Brown fumes and gusts of ice particles.

Shelter in the charred bordellos
and hollowed survivors, slated for demolition.
Missed quarters scammed from pay phones
and parking meters, handfuls of leftover pennies,
clattering sacks of aluminum.
Scattered men puddle at the Old Brewery Mission
wedged between romantic, cobbled evenings
and the grocers smelling like jerked trash and seafood.

II.

A taxi surge, burning co co ricos on the 'ti pains,
a billiards break, lechers slink out of the cinema.
"What's tonight's feature?"
            "Valley Vixxxens."
"Whiskey. With water this time."
Drunk girls in gladiator sandals,
ink tubes on the front steps,
a discarded skeleton key and Vogue super slims.
Three summits around the crater,
a boiling lake, prowling men in wolf masks—
are they feral? Do they bite?
Abandoned camps, tarp rooftops up there.
Drink supplicant, Christ save us from the eruption.
        "Four-fifty."
"Maudit crisse." The face of a dying queen
for fourteen years of labour
and not even one bride to show for it.
"Can I pay you in pretty words?"

        "Vous avez de fun?"

        "You're a creep."

A dress in *Twin Peaks* red, she sang at the Blue Dog
sweet sincerely and stank of it,
worse than the creep. A hand copped,
begging by the brisket in the window.
"Whiskey and water. Do you smell the sulphur?"
        "I smell three centuries of shit rising from the river
            and fried catfish. Four-fifty, plus tip."
Sorcery in the woods,
bodies on the slopes and in the bowers.
August odour on the street: barbecue and urine.
Sausages slip to the sidewalk at the fair.
"*Fordel* my lips. Can I buy you a drink?"

A hangover shake in the earth. The statues quiver.
Ash spumes behind the radio tower,
whistling shrieks as the Cocytus boils.

III.

Bicycles hang from the balcony rails,
leather jackets in the winter winds.
Everybody looks like album covers.

See the footnotes dragging along behind
like overstuffed luggage on clacketing wheels?
See fire-scarred genealogies dangling down past their heels.

Who drank all the red wine?
Who wrote the lyrics on the back of that hand?
And who rode the Bull at Chez Serge?

Under the viaduct, under the CP line,
there's a country carpentered
out of big dreams, big lands, big money.

IV.

Snowfall on Easter. They'll freeze when we break their windows.
They'll run shivering where they belong.
But every year they stink farther up the street.
Easter is the season of cold stones and gutter fires.
Let 'em know they can't crawl any higher
with their holy dirt still under their fingernails.

"Montréal serait toujours—"
Bombast at the point of decline.

"How come Joe doesn't move you out to St. Leonard?
You can't keep living in the city forever." Her mother,
who wonders why she married a prep cook,
why they won't move into the *città*
when they need that money to send their kid to an English school
and a good job in Toronto.

No more light-strung trees, no more ethnic chi-chi.
The mystery falls back against the clamour and fumes,
traffic, convenience, utilitarian structure and parking.
The muscle and bones both sing of all cities
stretches ahead in the north.
It's in the open air,
in the jackhammer and trundle
that they're building the new skyscrapers,
railroads from sea to sea.
Go north, without grimping.

V.

There is no place for panhandlers. Nobody walks.
There is no room between the buses, trucks,
bulldozers, snowploughs and broken slag.
There are rushing autoroutes, strip malls, block buildings,
thunder and lightning at ground level,
an automatized storm beyond the volcano.
People move in the comfortable isolation of their own designs.
Who, after all, would walk through the storm outside
where things are built and the city persists?
Life is a burning through and here the fire's fastest.

Where might a man live without facades and regulations,
without interference in his ambition,
free to torch and rebuild until he's gratified?
Even at the corner of Henri-Bourassa
there are a dozen régies and zoning laws,
municipal taxes, neighbourhood strangulation.

The boulevard stops, suddenly as it began,
by a river, with a view of the canopied strand.
She nibbles on a coffee bean, lying in the shade.
For now there are subtle excitements,
blood tides and flutters between two lovers,
lingering as they sense the south come between them,
their imminent return to disappointment and desire.
It's a game, now, to see how long they can stay
instead of eating and making, burning and fuelling
and wheeling down the boulevard
through the tempests of man's design, to succeed or survive.

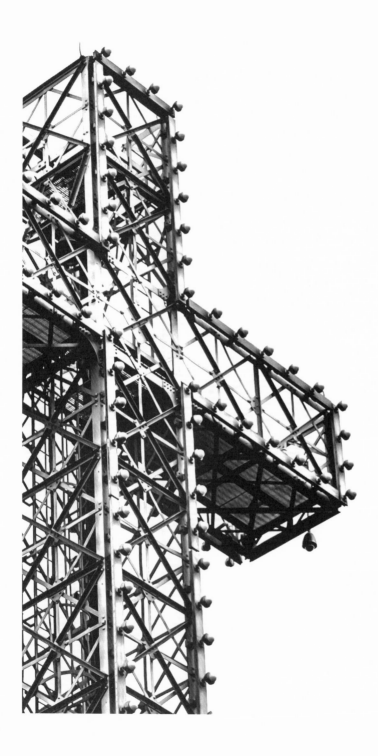

"CÔTE-VERTU"

The city only issued licenses for art. The houses had the most painstakingly carved mouldings and handcrafted roof tiles. The parks were peopled with sculptures until they were crowded as train platforms. The city's baristas were divided bitterly into two factions arguing endlessly and without anyone paying attention over the merits of blended and single-origin roasts. In that city, the sandwiches were made by sandwich artists.

"DU COLLÈGE"

In the suburbs of the imagination, monsters of the id pitch their starter homes.

"DE LA SAVANE"

The stars are closer in the space age.
The cave markings were scored by swamp light.

"NAMUR"

A proto-Sphinx without a question, an auroch's head on a lion's
   body, expecting an answer all the same.

"PLAMONDON"

Subcutaneous dirt streaked his hands.
Buses hovercrafted out of there.
Dusk panicked like people in a thunderclap
kicking sand up to the maple keys.
Searching for a friend, I recognized noses I no longer knew.

"CÔTE-STE-CATHERINE"

Whenever I'm in a part of town where I don't know the price of
   cigarettes
I start talking to the sidewalks and the bus stop billboards,
just repeating the words they tell me to repeat.
I scoop up some dried old foliage and opening my fist
three leaves, curled into lobster tails, twitch in the wind on my palm
like all the things that I know now that I'm not young enough to
   know everything.

"SNOWDON"

Punk smoking underground.
Angry father-figure sweat.
Ramen mistaken for street food.

"VILLA-MARIA"

The city announces its origins in three languages.
For years I thought Villa-Maria was Spanish.

"VENDÔME"

When all of my friends were gone, I went to find new ones.
They all owned knives and hid them in their boots.
They always had new kittens and they traded their diseases.
At Vendôme I left them to the soap operas of runaways.

"PLACE ST-HENRI"

Somewhere subterranean, a city's spirit is elusive
as the Gjallarhorn that calls a chase of ghost hounds.
Whether it wears long chiffon or a denim ensemble
depends on the station of the search.

"LIONEL-GROULX"

Haikus scroll along between strokes and AMT schedules.

"GEORGES-VANIER"

A tree in a cool blue park,
the light on a fountain underground.

"LUCIEN-L'ALLIER"

They're tearing the city down.
They won't rebuild.
The goblins of destruction were kept in Louis-Hippolyte
    Lafontaine's house.
They gnaw masonry away.
Their urine rots plasterwork
and the wasps born in their pustules disguise themselves as nails.
What they unearthed cannot be kept there,
not even by the hundred sentinels stationed by the gateway.

"BONAVENTURE"

Bonaventure: the meeting place of trains; a farewell; a rebuke to the
miserly.

"SQUARE-VICTORIA-OACI"

He guards the magnetic negative of financial institutions.
His single whip stance directs transit from office to metro.
He stands atop the dwindling treasures of the Banque Nationale
buried above the Orange Line.
He is their stone answer to the Anarchopanda,
a faceless sentry tethered to a paper paifang.

"PLACE-D'ARMES"

The city gates repulse dinners without table cloths.
Let the junk store doodads have their peace and quiet.
By midnight the ward falls under curfew;
rush home! Rush home before they lock the hutong doors.

"CHAMP-DE-MARS"

Amor vacui paves the parking lot.
You can only move when history's out of the way.

"BERRI-UQAM"

Berri-UQAM, the heart of the world,
ferry me eastward, delay me right here,
rob my wallet and dash my careers.

Drinkers and butterflies hurry down stairs.
Cinéastes stream into the station.
Their takeout containers steam in the air.

Berri-UQAM, au coeur du monde,
take me to Jarry Street, take me uptown,
take me past Sherbrooke, but leave me alone.

Students go bitterly; the library's quiet.
On platforms the newspapers love to collide.
Busy people wait for their blue train to arrive.

Berri-UQAM, under beggars and statues,
I've hopped your turnstiles, run for your sweepers.
Now hide me from my doctors, my creditors,
                                    my bosses, my friends.

"SHERBROOKE"

Plateau with many coloured walls I hear fiddles in your garrets and
   smell *bacalhau* de Terra Nova in an Acadian town
Plateau with many peaked mansards, devils' hands pry open your
   ceilings and drag students into flights over star-cold steeples
Plateau with many stairs you scaffold yourself for the window-
   washers who are sculptors and musicians and ex–adjunct
   professors whose ideas were sent packing from the castle on the
   hill
Plateau with a rigodon of statuary ziguezon-zinzon-ing as the
   nighthawks reach their houses
Plateau with ten thousand pigeons skewered on nail beds
Plateau with many fingers of ice haunting your portals
Plateau with your lungs full of firesmoke
Plateau with churches and shuttered synagogues and renovated
   patrimony
Plateau with harbour-slum plexes, mousers, lanterns, bull parades,
   protests, one-ways,
Plateau with teeth of shadows, pay no attention when they sneer
   at your puppet shows and menageries and whittle their envious
   darts out of tedium.

"MONT-ROYAL"

19h30 on the STM
it's full of everybody
sweating under tuques

that life

hoping the bus is on schedule
even in the weather

they've been to wherever
and booting themselves back home
they think of *dry* and *sort-of-warm*

they have all the reasons in the world
not to get out of bed tomorrow
to stop at station Mont-Royal
and walk the avenues far from their homes
until it is past midnight
and the city's heart is murmured by snow

"LAURIER"

Equip yourself with tedium on the adventure of your sobbing heart.
When your eyes recover their sight beneath the dreamworld,
you will recognize the shapes of monsters through the ceiling grates.
Cockroach, you will survive the illusion, even if you must eat your
   own
who choked and died on a sweet-smelling powder.

"ROSEMONT"

I searched amongst the bobos.
I hacked through fields of impossible things.
I snuck through fences and crossed forbidden pathways.
They promised klezmer bands and noise punk,
siguiriyas and glitter pop.
I believed in cafés and idleness
and super casual hookups.
I retraced the lengthy blocks.
I peered in every book in S.W. Welch.
Pong-like, I bounced up and down the viaduct,
though after I moved to Verdun,
I couldn't muster up the chutzpah to buy coffee
anywhere as frumpy-hip as Le Cagibi.

"BEAUBIEN"

City, let me give no two fucks and vanish.
Let me hole up in my bedroom and write my private hagiographies.
Never speak to me. Never send a glance
full of hate or puzzlement my way.
Make me scenery, sedimentary,
that barman in the Café Certa serving Dadaists.
Don't worry me with books or friends or pride.
Let me ask myself why I don't answer invitations.

"JEAN-TALON"

The fanfare of hangover horny.
The fanfare of *Tout le monde en parle*.
The fanfare of Doritos, Jack cheese and pickled jalapeños.

"JARRY"

Sit, Ubu, you've *Guignolled* your last penny out of Madelon.
Now *parle villerayais* your way out of Dadaists' jail.

"CRÉMAZIE"

An investigation: the crime was the canvas of ignorance spread
between the Transcanadienne and the church parks on the riverside.

"SAUVÉ"

I intruded; strangers have no right to visit cemeteries.
I stole other mourners' flowers to lay on my imaginary parents.

"HENRI-BOURASSA"

I skipped breakfast and fainted by Rivières-des-Prairies.
I staggered my retreat.

"CARTIER"

Under austero-liberal economic policies, the cost of reproducing
social stratification will be borne by the bottom classes.

"DE LA CONCORDE"

Higher transit fares, reduced peripheral service, and chronic affordable housing shortages occur as younger members of the social elite simultaneously perceive private automobiles as dirty, selfish and gauche.

"MONTMORENCY"

Single family homes are recast as socially demoralizing while suburbanizing poverty transforms cul-de-sac developments into "slums" that will ultimately be demolished just as contemporary tower developments reach their thirty- to forty-year life expectancy.

THE WORST TOUR GUIDE ON THE ISLAND

Before the ships sailed straight to Duluth,
Lenny came with a hint of coal particles.
It was around the corner that Chomedey
shot an Iroquois chief at the gates of Montreal,
one in the throat, one in the head, gun in each hand.
This is skid row. Was skid row,
unless the kids belting Sebastian Bach
in Steve's Music Store count.
Lenny lives up the way
in a modest duplex on the square.
Knock on his door around four in the morning
singing, "Everybody knows the ship is sinking,
and everybody knows your home address."
He'll stick his head over the sidewalk.
Never ask for tea and oranges.
He keeps a green bin up there
that he only empties in November.
He sits there eating Valencias,
brewing Earl Grey that he will never drink,
curling rinds between his fingers.

PLAGE MONTENEGRO

The day I found it closed, the Belle Guele lost its head
and the nosebleeds retreated to their stoops.
There would be no place to drink by buckets of snow
or smoke in a cold that's not quite outside.
New Year's and viande fumée blew tarpaulins aside
and dumped ashtrays into water damage.

When I pried at the door, the boulevard made eyes.
I am done. I will not go to Champs Bar.
Fun died on the curb. I give up on after-works,
drinking and hoping something will happen.
There is no such thing as St-Laurent anymore.
I cannot pay more than three dollars for my youth.

Adieu to the white sands, beach chairs and bikinis
(they must have hidden under the flannel).
Laku noc, old local. It was too cool for me,
anyway, lined up to actually pee.

Every time I walk the boulevard, my neck cranes
toward the window, straining for a light,
and the outline of a head shows like a phantom
contractor ripping up walls with grey hands.

Or the owner is measuring the window frame
against the width of the pool table, stumped.
The candles are out on the four-tops, on the bar,
though the out-of-season Christmas lights stay lit.

No one would notice its door click open at three,
no would hear me pull air from dry taps.
No one would mock my flatulent breaks, my scratches,
my losses, my backward smokes, my worn coat.
No one would recognize the outline of my face,
soured by whiskey and change on the street.

NO ONE GOES TO PRINCE ARTHUR ANYMORE

Is it because they can't tell the Casa Grecque
from the Cabane Grecque?
Because they drown in buckets of oversalted feta,
or they have lost their ways through white tablecloths
and folded napkins returning from the restrooms?

The hostesses stand out on the empty cobbles with smiles
about to break into back-rent tears
while the owners hunch over wineglasses
watching the Food Network, their shifty eyes darting to the street
accusing pedestrians passing to the metro,

"It's your fault, you ungrateful, hungry bastards;
my calamari never hurt an esophagus or soul."

The bartenders plant their palms on their polished bars
and wipe away their fingerprints,
afraid to besmirch the pristine towels on their shoulders
under the boss's cost-cutting glares.

No one goes to Prince Arthur anymore,
not unless there's a show at Café Campus,
not unless Pizza Exquise is still open.

Kalamatas grow fuzzy in their metal inserts,
red onions soften and stain quizzical fingertips,
the lamb meat sighs as it goes grey on its skewer.

Anna goes home early. Her section's seats are up already.
No one will come now.
The bartender has his glass, two hours to closing time.

She brushes through the ghosts of that couple
who spoke like they were in a library,

who didn't laugh once, though they split a baklava
and brought their own wine. She doesn't envy date nighters
who come in and look like they are splurging.
She wishes they would go somewhere else,
somewhere people laugh
and drink stupid cocktails and eat Korean tacos.

She hates when families come for birthday parties.
Wouldn't it be more fun to put on ties
and order St-Hubert chicken with a two-four of Bud
than make her stick sparklers into complimentary lava cake
and sing "Bonne fête" in her kindergarten voice?

She only wants to serve those businessmen at lunch
who drink too much wine for one hour
and like how fast the place serves brochettes on rice.
They don't seem to really care where they are.
They don't expect anything to be fun, or romantic or edible.

The last busker smiles at her with a smoke at his lips.
He rubs his arms and shivers instead of saying that it's too cold
    already,
that the sidewalk terrasses will go inside before Monday
and they won't see each other until May, or ever.

Everyone knows there won't be any turnaround.
Restaurants don't resurrect themselves, not monsters like these.
They burn down two days before the last busboy is fired,
they burn down and they never come back.

Anna rides the metro to Beaubien.
She opens up Kijiji to the food/bev/hosp pages
and types in "Vieux Port." She needs a new job,
before her landlord hears she's home.

CHAMP-DE-MARS

Last year's leaves fritter against the stumpy old wall,
the way mushrooms tremble when you throw them in a deep fryer.
When the city lost its wall, it was too small to build a ring road.

I don't want to share tonight with the kids in Place Vauquelin.
Can't they stub out their cigarettes and go steal extra-tall
tall cans they might pay for if they had the ID?

Can't I have it all to myself and pretend that the leaves
are the last red flowers laying siege to the new town,
to those towers that aren't quite tall enough to count as towers?

Can't I share my night with the statue of Vauquelin?
I'd sling my arm around him and show him to the ghost tours.
I'd say he'd come back to the ports of his all-or-nothing era.

I'd say he'd come back from France to find the sword
he'd thrown in the St. Lawrence, the guns of the *Atalante*,
the shadows he slipped through at Louisbourg.

NOCTURNE ON THE VIEUX-PORT CLOCKTOWER

No music, but subdued waves lick the pier.
No moon in the water but the clock tower's reflection.
Which water? No, the St. Lawrence,
but for a minute it was the bay, until
the uniform line of illuminated old buildings,
Vieux-Port, of course, and there isn't salt in the air.
The Viña Caballero is all mine, too,
with the clock tower's glint on the bottle.
There was company but not any wine by the other harbour.

The clock tower is white, la Giralda-like,
like the harbour clock tower in San Francisco,
too bright against the local gloom in the limestone,
the limestone with "le charme dangereux de la mort."
Those are the lights in Oakland, that white cantilever bridge.
No, the Jacques Cartier, and the South Shore,
and the bay was much bluer,
the St. Lawrence is a murkier ash, but both as black tonight.
Or maybe the Caballero has emptied into them.

Into my eyes, not the water. Like Catherine Tekakwitha's wine
spilling on the tablecloth, on the moon
and on the thighs of New Frenchwomen at dinner.
No wine ever stained San Francisco's tower.
There're eyes in red wine that have seen the bay harbour,
but not laughing and sad that the wine is singing so gaily.
Oakland is farther across the water and capped
with Oriental waves, not un Fleuve qui est dans les mots,
a river in the words like Caballero in the river.

The reflection of the clock tower on the water,
like a poem transfixed against passing—sure,
just passing. The clock is passing, too, unfixed.

41

No, seven o'clock on the water is five o'clock
on the tower. Isn't it? The Caballero has emptied from the bottle,
into my eyes and the river and the clock on the water,
not the moon. What moon? If there's no moon here,
is there a moon in San Francisco? No, I think.
There's no rue Nelligan in Oakland, either.

SKETCHES AT LE CAGIBI

He is not just annoying. He enunciates the French way
even when it isn't necessary. He says, "San 'Enri"
and means the neighbourhood of *Bonheur d'occasion*,
and not the Orange Line metro station.

CHINATOWN

When we go out, I never eat duck.
Or veal or lamb or rabbit.
The choicest meats are adorable.

The people in the noodle shop
are crammed at wooden tables.
De la Gauchetière has no bootleggers.

I order roast duck, broken joints and gristle,
fat-slick to slip down eager throats,
and I will choke just to please you.

Chinatown is comforting, especially
the mute TV shows. The lonely seem lonelier
with chopsticks. I can only dream of hidden menus.

SQUARE SIR-GEORGE-ÉTIENNE-CARTIER

In St-Henri the streets are more crooked than in other districts.
Even on the coldest nights, Christmas lights skate across the ice
in the fountain of Square Sir-George-Étienne-Cartier.
The city has torn down slaughterhouses for over a hundred years.
If old slaughterhouses tenant art galleries and beer breweries now
it doesn't change the Habs' playoff chances.
Whether people in the bars drink 50 or Export or St-Ambroise,
the team will tank halfway through the second round.

The trains in St-Henri are not shy of midnights,
even if there are canoes in the Lachine Canal,
even on school nights,
even during overtime.

The trains drag back and forth around the corner,
and the brakeman unhitches cargo half a kilometre away,
and drivers fume behind their wheels and mutter "Goddamn the CPR,"
and "Goddamn the Habs" when Radio-Canada announces Subban
    is in the box,
and Pacioretty has broken his neck again,
and Price lets one pass two minutes from the whistle
and fifteen until the train carries on to Pointe St-Charles.

RESTAURANT AA

The waitress scoops up menus,
the orders of those not swayed by more exotic hot dog dressings.
My tongue fails me again and again—I can't trust it.
I will lick the escalators at Place St-Henri
and let the blunt teeth sheer away betrayal.
Then truth will spout from my infected mouth,
yes, and I can tell the waitress I don't like relish!
It's too green, and the gravy is a little sweet.
If I could live either by the mountain or the Elpro building,
I would have to pick the closest to Restaurant AA.
Covet me, casse-croûtes, the way I covet you.
My faux-pas are breaking through the ice from below.
They are crawling out of the canal.
I must bolt the doors and rally the cook with his baseball bat
and arm the girls from next to Black Jack with shotguns.
The only illusions on Dream Street are VLT victories
and the appreciating value of real estate investments.
Many don't know this: When the *Chasse-galerie*
veered from the New Year's lights of Ville-Marie,
it crashed on the site of the Elpro.
The devil orders the cheeseburger combo every Sunday morning.
I only understand the waitress thirty seconds after she speaks.
I am a citizen of Trudeau's country:
half-lingual and sort-of tolerant.
St-Henri greeted me with a Shawinigan Handshake.
I only hope I won't end up rummaging through blue bins
after selling my degrees on Kijiji.
Even men who could be my boss eat the subs at Restaurant AA.
The waitress is everything I am not: competently indifferent.
I garble, like a man stumbling up and down active locomotive
    routes
and judging the different flavours of Blue Dry 7.2% and Blue Dry
    10.1%.
The tables are full, the plates are empty.

The waitress stares me down
and with a stern smile takes my water away.
Away. Enweille. Whatever. I hear it all the time.

SKETCHES AT LE CAGIBI

"But a poetry about burritos is regressively anti-revolutionary."

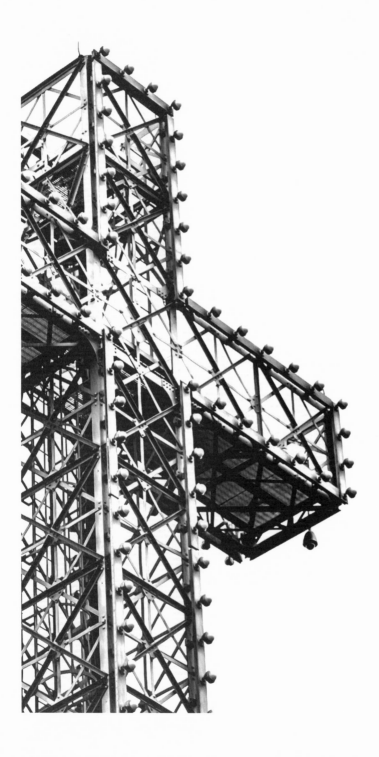

"SNOWDON"

A real city must have a Streamline Moderne cinema.

"CÔTE-DES-NEIGES"

Côte: a coast, a slope, a littoral, a rib,
an urban passage on a declivity.
The Snow-Coast. Snowyside.
Snowy Heights. Snow Hill Road.

"UNIVERSITÉ-DE-MONTRÉAL"

And what did you learn in school, they asked.
I learned that neon marks the class divide
between the two demographics that dress like 1992.

"ÉDOUARD-MONTPETIT"

Like spaghetti noodles in tomato sauce,
a student has to sit in ideas before they have any flavour,
but they will be cold after any longer than three minutes.

"OUTREMONT"

You cannot truly resent the rich without any affection for Mies-van-
der-Rohe car ports.

"ACADIE"

Acadji, O Acadji, je pleure the bayous of Île Saint-Jean,
the marais de Cap-Breton, les boisés and vallées of paroisse
    Lafayette,
the gulls driven ashore by the winter storms.
You can tell by the gullshit on Bombay Mahal
the date the ice will break in the harbour.

"PARC"

Death soared upward in the shape
of nine red onion rings.

"DE CASTELNAU"

The market is a frisson, a contact, a waste of time,
a market woman with eggs, a vintner, a flower girl,
a gourdmonger, a barbotte game all afternoon.

"JEAN-TALON"

Of all four lines, the Blue Line is Montreal's appendix.
Ostensibly useless, but a good home for gut flora.

"FABRE"

The Union of Postal Service Workers rebelled.
They unglued stamps and rewrote addresses.
They diverted all packages to Iqaluit and Cap-aux-Meules.
Home service was restored exclusively for nomads.

"D'IBERVILLE"

After the failure of the Gulf Stream, the Palais de l'Élysée
moved into The Marigny and leased back Louisiana
to weather out the global collapse.
When Premier Péladeau demanded, "Why not Le Plateau?"
President Hollande replied that the maple glaze
on Martin Picard's Pork Trotter Stuffed with Bison Tongue Foie
was an affront to the gastronomic heritage of France.

"ST-MICHEL"

Everyone rides the bus in a city of losers.

CÔTE-DES-NEIGES

Côte-des-Neiges,
                              your apartment will be raided again and again,
not by the SPVM, who know you run a dial-a-joint service,
who haul limbs out of your dumpsters and arrest your porn-star-illers,
not by your teenagers, who know better than to troll Cavendish Mall,
who have memorized the closing times of your shawarma shops
and pizza deliveries. It will not be by your pilgrims
                              dreaming under Easter eggshells,
who come in tour buses to polish their kneecaps on your wooden stairs,
porting their agonies from Catholic countries.

When the raiding squads come, the Snowdon delis will be deserted.
Young men will drop their paint cans, their murals will slip from
    their walls
undetected.
                    Metro will bar shut its automatic doors. Churros
                    will be rationed.
O Côte-des-Neiges, you will greet them all when the airport shuttle
terminates in your train stations. You were not bricked together
to turn your back on anyone, however much they will take with them
when they leave.
                    Your radiators were not installed to run for long.

Even when they stop to admire the maples in the park
by the Spanish and Portuguese Synagogue, they will betray you.
Even when they donate to the Segal Centre
or come back into town to dine at Pushap Sweets,
                                        they will betray you.
They will knock on your door through every night—
no one could keep their socks dry or their fingers warm
without your spare couch, the other side of your bed, your half-
    swept floor,
if you kept your chains latched against them.

ART SCHOOL DROPOUT

She screams at passing cars.
"Douche bucket" is her favourite word.
Her five-buckle boots are salt-stained and high.
She gave up on art.
She said, "Art won't save you."
She said, "Azure's just a tone of blue."
"Azure won't make god come to you."
She never got a job at an art store.
She never got a job at a record store.
She never plays her records late on work nights anymore.
She works in retail.
She throws out all her clothes
and never keeps her magazines.
She said, "Someday I'll fix shoes."

LA CARRETA

We come here when pizza night becomes every night.
We come here to pretend that nights off are special.
Most of my nights are off. I swill my ice water around.
Aromatic. I've settled for mistaking *pupusas* for romance.
I am hoaxing yucca into signs of devotion.
I've accepted station Beaubien for Paris,
and I only hope that she will still look at me
through the same *michelada*-tinted glasses of date night.

POPOCATÉPETL

The mountain is not the city's heart. A heart pulls cells back into it, replenishes, breathes. The mountain only pushes. Traffic runs carousels around. It repulses buildings, houses. The hospitals and mansions creeping up its slopes are fortresses of arrogance. They will surrender to the tectonics of ghosts. The mountain is the city's shadow. It is a nagging reminder of the time over Crescent Street. A dry-heave hangover at the end of Duluth. A heart doesn't appear in the gaps between rooftops, or in the catches and slips of streets and alleys. A heart doesn't lurk in the background like a bad memory.

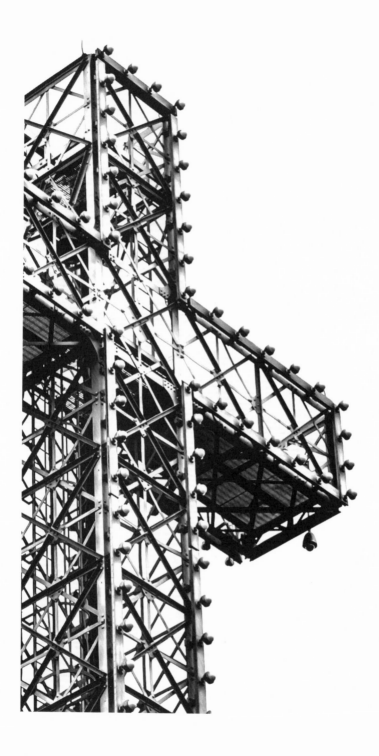

"HONORÉ-BEAUGRAND"

In contrast to the symbolic, monumental space of downtown, the geography of the *quartiers* inspires a mixture of banality and comfort, frustration and reassurance, from the grocery store to the diner to the bus stop to the apartment. Romantic sentiments in the neighbourhoods evolve out of personal narratives and not statist histories or the avant-garde of commercial fashions.

"RADISSON"

Trait woodrunner, Iroquanglais, pelter and point-blanketeer,
Radisson, protect this one-way trip,
clap my ears against the announcer tranquilly saying "fuck you."

"LANGELIER"

The natural dispersion of metro riders is double-spaced.

"CADILLAC"

The buzz of earbuds in the half-hearted straggle;
bashing your skull in to the drums of Julien Barbagallo.

"ASSOMPTION"

Trails of POM crusts,
croaks, sanglots, trickles of lost streams.
Delays kidnap the day.

"VIAU"

I choke on old words of mine.
My poems turn against themselves.
I can't convince myself of vatic qualities
when I hardly qualify as a bartender.

"PIE-IX"

Vernacular—adapted to the garage
cut into the ground, driveway sloped.
Articulated buses transport a message:
labour markets originate in displacement.

"JOLIETTE"

That woman in Rosemont didn't want you, anyway.
Don't listen to the screeches, howls.
Pipe down and sniff your Feliway.

"PRÉFONTAINE"

"Rape park," she said.
Skate park, I thought.
"Going home at night," she said.
"Alone," she said.

"FRONTENAC"

Now is the time to fumigate the bed bugs of the mind.

"PAPINEAU"

Make for the turnstile farthest from the ticket collector, timing yourself so that you arrive slightly before the person walking beside you. Placing hands on both gateposts around you, vault yourself over the turnstile and make for the escalator. Don't look back, it will only arouse suspicion. If you are slender, pull the turnstile as far back as it will go in the wrong direction, squeeze in, and pretend to flash your wallet at the OPUS scanner.

"BEAUDRY"

The photo booth encloses a few square feet of public space with the intimacy of the bedroom. The flimsy curtain that separates this ludic, romantic room from the indifferent cruelty of the metro is thicker than the door to a bathroom stall.

"BERRI-UQAM"

MR-63s are decorated with black-and-grey-speckled white seats
and bright diner-style lighting; the jolt of boarding an MR-73 comes
from the blue-and-orange colour scheme, the digital screens and
the increased number of passengers who look like intellectuals or
financiers.

"ST-LAURENT"

Somewhere underneath the lines, crowds, shows that burstpipe the
    sidewalk,
somewhere long after, there is still a land of cats and adolescents
sneaking under light bulbs
gagging on dragon's beard.

"PLACE-DES-ARTS"

Where I can never find the northbound 80.

"McGILL"

Scholars obfuscate their ignorance at any price.
They like to kill the daring, call them dangers.

"PEEL"

An oblique errand, a waft of dough and mozzarella.
A parking lot cuts to the bone of the place, scrapes an amnesia.

"GUY-CONCORDIA"

Someday they'll understand that "Head of Social Media"
isn't a job, it's a passion;
that tweeting is tougher than sonneteering
and tax returns are essays into our colonialized selves.

"ATWATER"

No one judges you downtown; they're too busy to care,
too used to mutterers and self-urinators
to mind a young man with a notebook.

"LIONEL-GROULX"

Station La-Petite-Bourgogne
Station Michaëlle-Jean
Station Rufus-Rockhead-et-Sa-Boîte-de-Nuit, Le-Paradis

"CHARLEVOIX"

The conductor had cabbage for hair. His chest was built out of Utica
shale and he had ice chips for eyes. He pointed with fiddle-string
fingers, stroked the bow where his tie meant to go.

"LASALLE"

The balcony extends the private into the public. Both part of the
common and elevated from it, the balcony preserves class elevation
in the street. "We are proud of this architectural peculiarity, where
each exit, no matter how high, permits unique access to exterior so
that every tenant may call her flat her home." And drink beer in her
underwear all summer long.

"DE L'ÉGLISE"

They say, if on a Sunday evening when there is hardly a noise or a
body in the station, you hear the vesper bells of Notre-Dame-des-
Sept-Douleurs, the next train will be a ghost train, and it terminates
in stations that were never built.

"VERDUN"

Pragmatic hatchets in the edicules create an oblique rhythm
out of the energies of Monday morning.

"JOLICOEUR"

Still aqueduct. Cerulean July.

"MONK"

Whenever I wave at Pic, it's always Pell who says to me,
"Your hands are too soft, what do you do all day?"

"ANGRIGNON"

Ultimate Frisbee and family barbecues hit an all-time low
around the time they found the head roasting in a tandoori summer.

THE COLLECTOR OF CENTRE-SUD

After Richard Suicide's Chroniques du Centre-Sud

All my life I've been collecting. Through putrid summers
and acid Boxing Days I've paced the blocks between Ontario
and Rachel, I've skirted the park with my red children's wagon
belting stovetops to refrigerators, I've dragged my swollen feet
up the hill to Sherbrooke and with my back to my haul
I've tiptoed down to my house again. I've caught bedbugs
and coquerelles, I've had lice in my beard and scabies on my
    kneecaps,
I've scraped my chest hair clear on scrap metal and bled
through my lizard-cracked hands over every appliance corner.
I've brushed away every splinter, I've yanked out every stray nail,
I've fixed, and tossed and rummaged, I've salvaged everything I
    could.
I've sat, and I've waited on everything I couldn't,
my eyes always fixed in the junk piles for that secret part.
Every day is garbage day. I cannot sleep on Moving Eve.
I'm worse than midnight movers and procrastinator packers.
I fidget, I strangle myself in blankets, I drown myself in beer
hoping to black out, but I can hear my old merchandise up the hill,
the broken blenders, the toaster ovens, the wrought iron fence posts,
the cracked signage, the second-hand start-overs.
I will take them back in, I will keep them here and mend them,
I will find them homes and shelter the ones with nowhere to go.
I am a bear, a dragon, a thief at the gates of the landfill of forgetting.
My paces are harried, I hear them on scaffolds, in pits, behind walls.
They're the dynamiters, the pile-drivers, the bulldozers.
They are everywhere, the demolishers, the thrower-outers
who want new things, new glass that smashes too quickly,
new memories of nothing. As if they haven't learned to forget,
they are always quitting and starting over.
I write their biographies in bric-a-brac, I am a preservationist,
a curator in the museum of obsolete purchases.

I keep a perfect catalogue. The cleaners cannot rob me.
They are taking away my front lawn, my sofa, my beer fridge,
my bicycle parts. I will take them to court,
I will collect each item they've condemned to the incinerators,
every issue of *Allô Vedettes*, every hand-stitched mass of paper,
every pipe and hubcap patterned with their unique neglect.
They cannot demolish my museums of themselves,
I keep a perfect inventory of tetanus shots and stains.

RUE DORION

I caught you hiding from your landlord, walked you to the Gare
d'autocar.
> A midnight move to Kitchener, your bags packed and your
> bugs gassed.
Maybe if I'd had a phone the frost patinas would not have crystallized
their way into your mental well being.
Maybe I could have offered your onion-nourished frame a place to
shake
> while the exterminators occupied your one-and-a-half.
Those days I couldn't tell a friend from a strip of used toilet paper.
> I was set dead on a new personality; ransacking my friends
> for traits.
You never said a word until later, when you learned to love butchery
and smokers,
> quoting Sufis in your hickory-scented meat locker,
a word about what a shithead I'd been.

You and I always shared one thing, though, and if it wasn't always
art,
> it was definitely always losing,
losing until the orchestra's toned down to the last silly klezmer
chord
> and you get to clop your hungry heels around.
We used my luggage to get your books into my place,
> everything from *Dune* to *Maldoror*.
Hauling ass to Berri-UQAM, you going, I won't miss this part of
town,
> the CrackDo's, Le Drugstore, waiting in station Papineau.
I read your books in your absence, until my mother drove them
home.
> In *Speed*, the narrator breaks down at the sound of locking
> doors.

THE METRO IS CLOSED BECAUSE YOU
FORGOT YOUR SCHOOL BAG ON THE SEAT

Dreary old rush hour, it's black and the snow is blue
and it's good that the doors at Promenades Cathédrale never close,
because the Great Antonio could not open them again.
People get dressed for the Bering Strait to go downtown Christmas
    shopping.
Behind those black collars and neck warmers I can't tell if they're
    lawyers or Dagwoods sandwich artists.
It's rush hour. They say it when the metro breaks down,
when the bus slams into a lamppost, when a truck skids sideways on
    the Mercier.
It's rush hour, they'll say it when the universe comes crashing down.
The end couldn't possibly happen at any other time of day.

Unemployment is Down

Day by day, I've been losing friends. Everyone I know is asking
    themself,
"How much longer, do you think?"
even if some of them were raised in NDG.
I can only live on tips and loans for so long
when every Christmas gets me closer to a high school reunion.
In my own voice I started hearing Toronto's favourite phrase:
    "What a loser."
I have seven-and-a-half months.
No one told me I could be a loser anywhere, even English Canada.

It's Five-Dollar Mortadella Month

Every time I go to Dagwoods I remember a poem about tomatoes,
and I think that onions are giants' tears buried in the earth.
Lettuce remains a salmonella liability.

I'll never know Neruda's opinions on banana peppers.

I ask for extra: those salamander tongues taste like volcanoes
and erotic feelings in Communist countries.

There are evenings when rush hour never wants to end.
At Dagwoods I look up from the paper;
no one is downtown. They didn't want me to see them go.

One sandwich artist berates another for coming late,
and for leaving three heels of Mortadella last night.
The tomatoes aren't quite ode material anymore.

STE-CATHERINE STREET

The néonistes scatter blind buckshots through flash mobs and light
    streams
and the zeroistes have slunk themselves to exhaustion with
    phantoms and words in their mouths like clumps of chewed
    cardboard
gangs of nobodies throb sliced thumb-like down the sink
and stain the place des arts basin luminous for the carnival season
stain bookshops and cafés the bars the malls the cinémathèques the
    strip joints the burlesque
the 2-22 all glass and dreaming the Théâtre Monument-National
    frosted over in promise the UQAM béton brut the gay dives the
    McDos the bridge and the churches
Ste-Catherine street is the job of the city builders
jobbers bartenders retailers barkers nuns short orderers beam
    balancers
whatever gets heaped in and barfed out everyone on Ste-Catherine
    stokes a steam ship sailing down to the Gulf.

COCK AND BULL

But I wasn't listening to the man on his stool.
Who knew you could shoot crème de menthe with brandy?
Who knew when my ex would walk in, when my friend would barf?
Not tonight, I prayed, and asked for paper towels.

I scrubbed down the bar top with beer.
I don't care what the snobs say.
You can see your face in sticky red cedar
with two heavy coats of Belle Guele.

When they asked me to leave, I was already dancing
on the wobbly table, tripping in my sudsy laces.
Before we were gone, I knew my ex had new dives
where the benches didn't smell like frosh week love.

I thanked the man on his stool for the brandy. He said,
"By the time you're fifty-one, you accept that gout still exists.
By the time you're seventy-one, you regret the little things,
like ordering garden salads, and photography exhibits."

DOWNTOWN NIGHT IN JANUARY

"la grande St. Catherine Street galope et claque
dans Les Milles et une nuits des néons"

Who called this exile? This is joy in the season of silence,
the season of salt cakes, boot crust, and beer hunkered in taverns.
Cold is the feeling that you have not died,
not yet, and do not want to die, breathing knives
like pine trees bristling against snowstorms
and snowbanks heaped on their boughs.

I thrive in the frost. I jig knee-deep and drunk
and fling the snow piled up on my hat.
It's so heavy on my head, so much lighter as it falls.

ON McGILL AVE

You passed me on McGill Ave, but I turned my head
because you were yelling, and your hands waved the way they do
when no amount of talking could finish what you had to say,
and you were with your ex with whom you only just leased
a place on Esplanade, with bay windows, wood floors
and pipes that protested like the *cacerolazo*.
That was in September, it was summer still
though the students rushed, some lost and some haggard
from familiar classrooms and dreaded professors.
I was scrambling from one bookstore to another
without luck, but you didn't ask, so I didn't ask your ex
why she would move to Toronto like all of them
who couldn't bear the wet, riparian winters,
or living in bohemia forever.
Neither of us moved here to forget our friends
but to trade insomnia for 24/7.
Today, I know more of the city's many sides,
its second floor secrets, its hiding places, cellars,
its dead-end lanes and afterhours lofts
and why, when you see a friend on McGill Ave,
running late already after too many lunch beers
when he's arguing publicly with an ex,
you might pretend not to see him if he's missed you.

KRAMPUS CAROL OF DE MAISONNEUVE

On the night before the last night of exams
the students pillow their foreheads on Klaebers and keyboards.
Their Facebooks stall on tinsel living rooms
and family pets. In Al-Taib two men sip Cokes.
Mushroom bits and tomato stain their paper plates.
They have their coats on, watching misplays of the month.

No one holds his scarf against the snow that seeks the sky again.
No one gasps and grunts and pokes his frozen nostrils.
Even the Krampus is curled up with his schnapps.
Even the abominable tuck themselves in their beds.

THE FLÂNEUR

He has an ear so sensitive he can tell you which block you were
    born on.
He can name the intersections of sewer grates through his shoe soles
and which buried stream courses through its drainage channels.
He waltzes mannequins down Sherbrooke past Christmas tunes and
    concierges.
He is the confidant of every pigeon in Place Norman-Bethune.
In his palm he taps the rhythm of the flicker of each light bulb on
    the Metropolis marquee.
When he whispers his love to the empty alleys he mouths the shape
    of the island.
He can trace your erotic fantasies from the lines on your forehead to
    your crow's feet.

The history of the sidewalk patio aches his back molars.
Sudden right turns fray his daydreams.
He wears away the heels of his socks.
He is on a forced march to a centrifugal destination.

FRIENDSHIP COVE

She said blondes were for pussies. What she meant was beer.
The band dressed like Riquer figures, and three out of four played
    keyboard.
Syrup stickied the walls and drew the hobgoblins from their
    bedrooms.

After that summer the noise bands came, and we sucked our shoes
    out of the punk.
The food at Moe's stayed the same, and the Seeburg Wall-O-Matics
    still never worked.
We went to Il Motore and pretended not to know our old classmates.

She couldn't stop her favourite bands from breaking up.
She just stopped listening. "New" left our vocabulary.

No one plays at Friendship Cove.
Cushfield and Wakeman wait for Graham Van Pelt's last chorus to
    rattle the aluminum.
They fear the ghosts of the fashionably dressed so much more than
    zoning committees.

I wore that blazer that's lost its shape and smells like falling asleep
    on the subway.
She said you can only hide at Moe's until dawn drags you out by its
    teeth
and in the morning rush you're nauseous with your own mildewy
    insomnia.

The bottom of the bottomless coffee is full of goblins and the ends
    of things.

FARINE FIVE ROSES

The towers pull the overcast close.
The snow is grim in the gothic banking district.

GAP

He hunkered, in mission dormitories,
warmed by hypodermic needles
and Dilaudid pills, living on Big Macs,
riding metro trains through the season of death.

The city is a loneliness. But one must have friends,
sixty dollars a day for Dilaudid,
living in judgment and evictions.
Loneliness is a luxury of the employed.

It rains through the city
on the vagrants with guitars.

Compromise is easier.
His face groans mangled from the cover of his book,
drunk, howling desperate emails, beatings,
losers, hospitals, cruelties.
The judgment of the dead hangs over me
while I plot careers and pizza Mondays.

He could not read his battered poems
written on wet papers riding metro trains.
The city's hate blew in
behind their jeers.
You're a junky. You're a fucking junky.

He is the judge. Now he is the hateful one.

I cannot uncover from his books and cynic laughter
his blood blooms and needles,
his days of vagrants with guitars.

AROUND THE OLD SEVILLE

The alley cats recite Jacques Prévert lyrics.
The students sing "I'd rather be a doctor than flip burgers at
    McDee's."
The townhouses question the meaning of being in reinvestment
    cycles.
The bistros sneer at basketball sneakers
and the shish taouk shops wail wind through the cedars.
The bars make promises they never keep.
The bookstores hush up their secrets.
The high-rises talk about modern life as if 1968 never happened.
The brake lights are unanimous: no, no, don't go.

GREY DONKEYS ON THE ROAD TO EL AZIB

Smoke sneaks through the hinges on the door.
The students and locals baccarat evenings to old age,
sparking coals and nursing coffees.

A woman makes *lahmajoun* in her shop window.
She thumps dough to wood,
ignores passersby all afternoon.

The Ali Basha's on Peel went for a Jeita Grotto look.
The view is more newscast at six,
the rooftop green screen showing midnight rush hour.

Most nights end at Al-Taib.
They salt the streets with *zaatar* here.
A man waits for every morning watching highlights on RDS.

ALLEY CAT IN WINTER

Let the others nap under parked cars.
I've seen plenty startled and crushed.
I don't mind, let the snow build flake by flake.
Others watch it swirl,
others paw at back doors.
The humans fly arcs of snow over their fences
thumping softly into snow like nightfall at Christmas.

MY CAT AS SEEN BY AN ALLEY CAT

The upstairs neighbour is a simpleton.
He broke his talon on a tree stump;
as he tensed in the shadows his own bell startled him.

I napped with one eye open.
He is simple and does not like me,
but his people came calling for him.
Roasted chicken on a summer night rich with odours.

ALLEY CAT DISTEMPERED

High summer, abandoned ones again,
hungry ones and conspiratorial ones,
they cross the boundaries I have laid out,
I catch them thieving from my dish.
I am like a summer storm;
if I am short-lived,
my ferocity will be hard to forget.

TABAGIE CHEZ MOI

I would open a depanneur just to watch kung fu films all night,
and as the young apprentice lands his first blow on Pai Mei
the local teenagers could boost the six-packs and Molson quarts
without fear of baseball bats or Tiger style or police reports.

Kids from as far as Ville-Émard would hear of jacked wine racks,
Tremblay fifteeners, amaretto bottles and stacks on stacks of
    Pringles.
Even my jerky and Oh Henry!s could vanish unseen
while the cat food collected roach shit and the cream expired.

At Tabagie Chez Moi, Shaolin shadowboxers duel between the
    empties.
Only the cigarettes are safe from the boosters and sticky-fingered.
The paying customers will wave their money in my face for nothing.
I wave my Wonder Bread goodbye as it's carted through the snow.

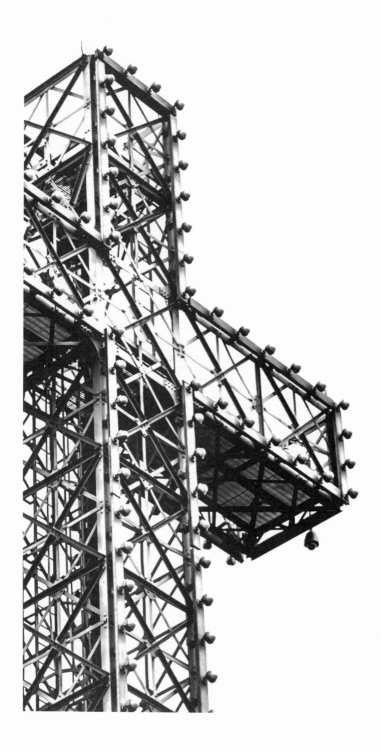

"BERRI-UQAM"

The "not-a-priority" commuter gets there one way or another,
by crook or by standing and waiting half an hour, freezing, then
sweating, swaying, bumping, crowding, cursing, standing, fainting,
tripping, frowning and finally freezing again.

"JEAN-DRAPEAU"

Man the scorpion.
Man in victory.
Man in protest.
Man of the earth, the alien,
the maker of alien-things.

"LONGUEUIL-UNIVERSITÉ-DE-SHERBROOKE"

The longest line on the STM is the Yellow Line.
Leaving the island is like leaving behind hope
and letting go of dietary idealism.

A NEW YORK CITY CHRISTMAS

I am entertaining winter, and I will make her cocktails
from the mini-bar. It is almost Christmas
and you are in another borough, past the Bronx.
The frenzy of bags and credit cards sputters
as the night deepens with lonely siren blasts
and the ocean roar of mechanical life.

You must be alone, by the useless radiator
in our apartment by the river.
I have winter here, cool and charming,
over the quivering blocks of the Upper West Side,
unsteady and fragile though they slowly sink Manhattan.
She does not like my sidecars.

Winter is the season of love. In Times Square
this evening the lights were even lonelier in the cold.
In Times Square it is hard to believe that I am alive.
Now Amsterdam is vacant, though taxis
and rent-weary pedestrians pass inaudibly,
and in those many towers someone must watch television.

Come through the Catskills, we can go to beaches
along the boardwalk in summer and watch mermaid parades.
Come, ride the Sea Beach Line in seashells,
with a shark net skirt, a starfish painted on your cheek.
We'll eat pretzels and hot dogs for dinner.
They roast chestnuts in December.

I will bring you postcards from MoMA
and scribble lyrics on the backs of them.
Winter is a motherfucker, a longshoreman
bellowing through the bottom of his rye. Here,
she's the longshoreman's daughter,
and he will slug my teeth out three-by-four.

MONTRÉAL

City of breakdowns, city of leaving, city of failure,
city of matadors, losers, gamblers, clowns,
city of bridge-builders and Sulpicians, DPs and revolutionaries,
city of schemers, hoarders, tattoos, idlers,
city of *siddurim*, psalms, masses, odes, missals, *adhans*,
city with fingers of frozen rain, fingers of church spires, neon fingers
    and aircraft warning lights.
City, keep me standing. I need you to keep me standing another day,
    another year.
City riveraine, I can hear the carillon they never installed in the Tour
    de l'Horloge,
I hear your parle fluvienne tearing its anglophonic syllables apart on
    the Rapides de Lachine,
I hear wails and curses, laments and pleas,
the metronome of pile drivers reverberating through the ceiling,
I hear the ice cracking—I hear the rites of spring rustling in closets,
I hear an orchestra of potholes moaning,
the urns of Notre-Dame-des-Neiges rattling in their mausoleums,
I hear the staircases tightening around my neck
and the manifestos of CEGEP students, their *vuvuzelas* and drums,
the clatter of batons keeping time on polycarbonate,
a fox, creeping through the underbrush of Westmount manors.
Second-hand city, recycled in vinyl record shops, antiquarian
    bouquinistes,
I salvage your morning coffee stains from Renaissance,
the stubborn pheromones of impromptu sex on your old sofa at
    Value Village.
I judge your hemlines and cracked leather in the *tandlmark* friperies
where you keep all your junk and kitsch,
I hoard your old books for their marginalia,
VHS tapes, to see which scenes have been worn down by rewinds,
I buy your paraphernalia by the kilo,
I take it to my scrapyard and build trash sculptures
out of commemorative Expo plates and Olympics '76 tuques.

By the time a monument is built the moment is already over.

I'll twist them into Pics and Pelles and post them on my balcony
stairs,

I will teach them language so they know to say,

when the stranger from the river asks, "Is Ville-Marie complete?"

"No, not yet, not yet." Never yet, I tell my Pics and Pelles,

or he will drown us, a substrate set piece,

fish food and floaters from scum-sucker faubourg to the mansions of
the koi.

SUD-OUEST

The city hides from me. It is frightened.
It turns its shoulder, lets me know
I am not welcome to stumble shouting from its buses
or spit on its cab drivers grubbing nickels
from my pockets. It will not keep me
safe from dawns spent puking on subway cars.
Others fling their styrofoam and donut boxes,
others may rap on drive-thru windows,
pick beer bottles from blue bins
and rattle sacks of empty cans.
Others are allowed under winter's intimate shrouds,
but I can't join them, I can't see the steeples
or the silos or the clocks on the market
through the snow from the Ville-Marie this morning.